READ THIS BOOK.

Author: KAYING KHANG

TODAY'S DATE:
FEBRUARY 9, 2024.

THIS BOOK IS FOR
YOU WHO SEEKS A
SELF-HELP BOOK.

READ ON TO DISCOVER SOMETHING
OLD OR NEW FOR YOUR MIND AND LIFE.

Once Upon a Time in a Land Long Ago, there lived a man and his wife and his family and childrens.

A world where everything matters and only KINDNESS is the key to ultimate success and freedoms on Earth.

There was a MISSION for all Humans to come down to Earth by Birth for a Vision we see and know and do! KARMA good and bad endows all.

It is eminent to say that 'YO WHATS UP BITCH!' "YOU SEE I GOT MONEY" "NO MAN IM BROKE!"

AND THERE WAS ONCE A FAIRY TALE.
But that Dream died when True Love Prevailed.

And now ancient as history, this book lives to tell you the WAYS to LIFE.

What is LIVING you might ask? It is not just breathing Air or Oxygen but it is in sense, the freedom to live with your life values in Good Man's worlds. With "pursuit of life, love, liberty and freedom."

Now as a child, I did and do PLEDGE MY ALLIGIANCE. I am glad to be part of this world and a country of love and freedom.

But I worry everyday because I'm broke. HOW DO I GET RICH NOW AT 43 NOW THAT OPPORTUNITIES ARE AT STAKE??? 2024 IS MY YEAR.

I MIGHT NEVER BE RICH BUT I HOPE I
MAKE SOME INCOME. SO I WROTE THIS
BOOK.

I have no mentor except this voice on youtube
atm. 'FINANCIAL PROSPERITY IS MY
STATE OF BEING. I AM GRATEFUL FOR
THE ABUNDANCE THAT SURROUNDS ME.
I AM READY FOR THE …. THE UNIVERSE
…I AM A MONEY MAGNET ATTRACTING
WEALTH EFFORTLESSLY. … FINANCIAL
OPPORTUNITIES….I AM A POWERFUL
CREATOR OF WEALTH AND SUCCESS. …I
ATTRACT WEALTH BY ALIGNING MY
ACTIONS WITH MY GOALS. I AM OPEN
TO RECEIVING UNLIMITED PROSPERITY.
…"

THERE that was the KEY TO WEALTH YOU
JUST READ AND HEARD but it is not the
only way.

MONEY IS FREE TO RECEIVE AS
RESOURCES MADE WERE FREE. ON
EARTH AND BY HUMANS.

ONLY THE BEARED LABOR MADE
THINGS COSTED MONEY BECAUSE
SOMEDAY BROUGHT IT OUT TO US ALL
BY THEIR HANDS AND BRAINS AND
WORK, LABORS.

SO THUS OUR LITTLE FREE WORLD
COSTS MONEY BECAUSE WE ARE ALL
STRANGERS AND COULD NOT YET GIVE
FREELY BACK ONE DAY YET TODAY
EVEN IN YEAR 2024 WORLD WIDE.

THUS MONEY HAD TO BE THE LETTER
OF TRUST TO MAKE THE BARTER PAID
TO ITS SOURCES THAT BROUGHT US
THRU FRUIT AND WORK, THE LABOR

THAT BROUGHT US ALL THESE
BEAUTIFUL THINGS IN THIS
WONDERFUL WORLD(s).

In my world, I got everything for free yet I had
to pay things with money that I got for free but
now that im 43 I need more money. I DO
WANT TO BECOME A TRILLIONAIRE! But
this is only a DREAM for now.

It is hard to be RICH because I do not want to
be a target to be outlisted or a public profile
where Poparrizzis follow me daily. Gosh that's
no life at all! Anyone?

Wont even be able to walk into the Mall no
more to buy my shoes or clothes than!
Hahahaahah that's not good.

So this book is intended to help you and all everythone to become RICH millions billions Trillions QuadtripleTrillions!!!??? Who knows….we can do this right? People mastered the skills of being rich. Why not you and me.

But the secret is this kids! MONEY WAS GIVEN TO HALF THE RICH TO BE KEPT RICH FREELY. Nobody told me that government and countries can give people money to be rich by GRANTS, LOANS, INCOME, PROFITS! ETC….

WELL THE KEY IS TO WEALTH IS ABUNDANCE TO LIFE IS SECURITY TO LOVE AND LIVE WITH FEES FREEDOME.

"WHO WANTS TO BE A LITTLE millionaire?" Some KIDS FIGURED IT OUT. SOME NEVER GAVE THEMSELVES A FAIR

CHANCE SO THIS BOOK SAYS IF YOU CAN THINK IT, IF YOU CAN DREAM AND BELIEVE IN IT AND NO ONE IS HURTING YOU, YOU ARE FREE TO MAKE BILLIONS MILLIONS TRILLIONS BUT PEOPLE JUST DON'T KNOW ALL THAT MONEY FOR WHAT?

Heck I still don't know…im just trying to find a way to pay our mortgage and get food and buy a cheap car I can drive again with paid insurance, etc…im the most broke joke blow it all lost B in America. I swear. Man….my life is hard. Because people are hating on me with their conspiracy Joni R and them drugging me 20 years for bad records of mental illness… I thought I was second class medicine/ citizen being Hmong so I accepted their tortures on my life 20 years but today I write my book to tell the world, WE CAN ALL BE BILLIONAIRES.

THEY KNEW IM SET TO BE RICH BUT NOW IM DIRT POOR BECAUSE THEY DRUGGED ME TOO LONG IN DRUGS THAT WILL RETARD ME AND IM WORKING WITH TIME NOW BEFORE MY LITTLE BODY GIVES OUT TO THEIR DRUGS ANYMORE! JONI R THEY ARE ENDANGERING MY LIFE WITH MENTALLY ILL DRUGS ON PURPOSE IN THEIR TARGET TO WRONGFULLY KILL ME BECAUSE JONI had sex with my brother on accident in Nekoosa WISCONSIN when we are in Elementary school playgrounds 3x 4 x Joni told me that day on the play ground. Heck I did not even know I had a brother til later. I am sorry okay. I'm sorry. Please do not hurt me anymore Joni Redepeening/Reimber aka Lyndsey.

With Love,
Kaying Khang.

So??? The right path to "financial success?"
That's this:

1. Either get a JOB work by the hour for money get paid x days or a week(s) later
2. Or Work for somebody or make your own companies to build somethings to offers some services and sales from those two options for your company.
3. Get loans to run a business. Business can be in ANY LEGAL SECTORS / INDUSTRIES. YOU can DREAM here and make your visions become true but I advise do it legally. That is do not steal, no crimes and opcn run your operations legally to profit sales and revenue into your business. For profit or nonprofit type businesses. Google it up: the difference between a profit or nonprofit business.

To me? They are the same things PROFITS and NONPROFITS. EXCEPT in their BOOK

KEEPING ACCOUNTING RECORDS ARE CLASSIFIED JUST A LITTLE DIFFERENLY. THEY BOTH MAKE MILLIONS BILLIONS DOLLARS OR can both be in DEFICIT TOO/ loss incomes.

THERE THAT'S THE KEY TO MAKING MONEY FOR YOURSELF!

NOW, WHAT KIND OF CAR DO YOU WANT TO DRIVE AS A MILIONARIE?

HMMM I ALWAYS THOUGHT IT THE LAMBOURGHINI BUT I THINK THAT'S MADE IN ITALY AND IM NOT SURE EVERYONE WANTS TO DRIVE THAT CAR RIGHT???? JK, MYSELF I DON'T WANT TO DRIVE THAT KIND OF CAR ITS TOO HARD.

EVEN IF I WERE RICH I'LL DRIVE AN OLD NICE IMPORTS PLEASE DON'T BAN

THESE CARS NO MORE. BRING IT BACK
THE GOOD OLD DAYS.

WITH LOVE,
KAYING KHANG

MY DREAM DID NOT COME TRUE YET.
IM TRYING. HAHAHAHAHAAHAHHAHA
BILLLIONS OF DOLLARS IS COMING TO
YOU AND ME. AHAHAHAHA MAKE
MONEY FLOW TO ME AND YOU! BE
SECURED. FOLLOW YOUR HEART!

LOVE,
PEACE,
LOVE,
PEACE,
LOVE, PEACE. THE END. MAKE MONEY!

READ THIS BOOK.

Author: KAYING KHANG

TODAY'S DATE:
FEBRUARY 9, 2024.

THIS BOOK IS FOR
YOU WHO SEEKS A
SELF-HELP BOOK.

READ ON TO DISCOVER SOMETHING
OLD OR NEW FOR YOUR MIND AND LIFE.

Once Upon a Time in a Land Long Ago, there lived a man and his wife and his family and childrens.

A world where everything matters and only KINDNESS is the key to ultimate success and freedoms on Earth.

There was a MISSION for all Humans to come down to Earth by Birth for a Vision we see and know and do! KARMA good and bad endows all.

It is eminent to say that 'YO WHATS UP BITCH!' "YOU SEE I GOT MONEY" "NO MAN IM BROKE!"

AND THERE WAS ONCE A FAIRY TALE.
But that Dream died when True Love Prevailed.

And now ancient as history, this book lives to tell you the WAYS to LIFE.

What is LIVING you might ask? It is not just breathing Air or Oxygen but it is in sense, the freedom to live with your life values in Good Man's worlds. With "pursuit of life, love, liberty and freedom."

Now as a child, I did and do PLEDGE MY ALLIGIANCE. I am glad to be part of this world and a country of love and freedom.

But I worry everyday because I'm broke. HOW DO I GET RICH NOW AT 43 NOW THAT OPPORTUNITIES ARE AT STAKE??? 2024 IS MY YEAR.

I MIGHT NEVER BE RICH BUT I HOPE I MAKE SOME INCOME. SO I WROTE THIS BOOK.

I have no mentor except this voice on youtube atm. 'FINANCIAL PROSPERITY IS MY STATE OF BEING. I AM GRATEFUL FOR THE ABUNDANCE THAT SURROUNDS ME. I AM READY FOR THE …. THE UNIVERSE …I AM A MONEY MAGNET ATTRACTING WEALTH EFFORTLESSLY. … FINANCIAL OPPORTUNITIES….I AM A POWERFUL CREATOR OF WEALTH AND SUCCESS. …I ATTRACT WEALTH BY ALIGNING MY ACTIONS WITH MY GOALS. I AM OPEN TO RECEIVING UNLIMITED PROSPERITY. …"

THERE that was the KEY TO WEALTH YOU JUST READ AND HEARD but it is not the only way.

MONEY IS FREE TO RECEIVE AS
RESOURCES MADE WERE FREE. ON
EARTH AND BY HUMANS.

ONLY THE BEARED LABOR MADE
THINGS COSTED MONEY BECAUSE
SOMEDAY BROUGHT IT OUT TO US ALL
BY THEIR HANDS AND BRAINS AND
WORK, LABORS.

SO THUS OUR LITTLE FREE WORLD
COSTS MONEY BECAUSE WE ARE ALL
STRANGERS AND COULD NOT YET GIVE
FREELY BACK ONE DAY YET TODAY
EVEN IN YEAR 2024 WORLD WIDE.

THUS MONEY HAD TO BE THE LETTER
OF TRUST TO MAKE THE BARTER PAID
TO ITS SOURCES THAT BROUGHT US
THRU FRUIT AND WORK, THE LABOR

THAT BROUGHT US ALL THESE
BEAUTIFUL THINGS IN THIS
WONDERFUL WORLD(s).

In my world, I got everything for free yet I had
to pay things with money that I got for free but
now that im 43 I need more money. I DO
WANT TO BECOME A TRILLIONAIRE! But
this is only a DREAM for now.

It is hard to be RICH because I do not want to
be a target to be outlisted or a public profile
where Poparrizzis follow me daily. Gosh that's
no life at all! Anyone?

Wont even be able to walk into the Mall no
more to buy my shoes or clothes than!
Hahahaahah that's not good.

So this book is intended to help you and all everythone to become RICH millions billions Trillions QuadtripleTrillions!!!??? Who knows….we can do this right? People mastered the skills of being rich. Why not you and me.

But the secret is this kids! MONEY WAS GIVEN TO HALF THE RICH TO BE KEPT RICH FREELY. Nobody told me that government and countries can give people money to be rich by GRANTS, LOANS, INCOME, PROFITS! ETC….

WELL THE KEY IS TO WEALTH IS ABUNDANCE TO LIFE IS SECURITY TO LOVE AND LIVE WITH FEES FREEDOME.

"WHO WANTS TO BE A LITTLE millionaire?" Some KIDS FIGURED IT OUT. SOME NEVER GAVE THEMSELVES A FAIR

CHANCE SO THIS BOOK SAYS IF YOU CAN THINK IT, IF YOU CAN DREAM AND BELIEVE IN IT AND NO ONE IS HURTING YOU, YOU ARE FREE TO MAKE BILLIONS MILLIONS TRILLIONS BUT PEOPLE JUST DON'T KNOW ALL THAT MONEY FOR WHAT?

Heck I still don't know…im just trying to find a way to pay our mortgage and get food and buy a cheap car I can drive again with paid insurance, etc…im the most broke joke blow it all lost B in America. I swear. Man….my life is hard. Because people are hating on me with their conspiracy Joni R and them drugging me 20 years for bad records of mental illness… I thought I was second class medicine/ citizen being Hmong so I accepted their tortures on my life 20 years but today I write my book to tell the world, WE CAN ALL BE BILLIONAIRES.

THEY KNEW IM SET TO BE RICH BUT
NOW IM DIRT POOR BECAUSE THEY
DRUGGED ME TOO LONG IN DRUGS
THAT WILL RETARD ME AND IM
WORKING WITH TIME NOW BEFORE MY
LITTLE BODY GIVES OUT TO THEIR
DRUGS ANYMORE! JONI R THEY ARE
ENDANGERING MY LIFE WITH
MENTALLY ILL DRUGS ON PURPOSE IN
THEIR TARGET TO WRONGFULLY KILL
ME BECAUSE JONI had sex with my brother
on accident in Nekoosa WISCONSIN when we
are in Elementary school playgrounds 3x 4 x
Joni told me that day on the play ground. Heck
I did not even know I had a brother til later. I
am sorry okay. I'm sorry. Please do not hurt
me anymore Joni Redepeening/Reimber aka
Lyndsey.

With Love,
Kaying Khang.

So??? The right path to "financial success?"
That's this:

1. Either get a JOB work by the hour for money get paid x days or a week(s) later
2. Or Work for somebody or make your own companies to build somethings to offers some services and sales from those two options for your company.
3. Get loans to run a business. Business can be in ANY LEGAL SECTORS / INDUSTRIES. YOU can DREAM here and make your visions become true but I advise do it legally. That is do not steal, no crimes and open run your operations legally to profit sales and revenue into your business. For profit or nonprofit type businesses. Google it up: the difference between a profit or nonprofit business.

To me? They are the same things PROFITS and NONPROFITS. EXCEPT in their BOOK

KEEPING ACCOUNTING RECORDS ARE CLASSIFIED JUST A LITTLE DIFFERENLY. THEY BOTH MAKE MILLIONS BILLIONS DOLLARS OR can both be in DEFICIT TOO/ loss incomes.

THERE THAT'S THE KEY TO MAKING MONEY FOR YOURSELF!

NOW, WHAT KIND OF CAR DO YOU WANT TO DRIVE AS A MILIONARIE?

HMMM I ALWAYS THOUGHT IT THE LAMBOURGHINI BUT I THINK THAT'S MADE IN ITALY AND IM NOT SURE EVERYONE WANTS TO DRIVE THAT CAR RIGHT???? JK, MYSELF I DON'T WANT TO DRIVE THAT KIND OF CAR ITS TOO HARD.

EVEN IF I WERE RICH I'LL DRIVE AN OLD NICE IMPORTS PLEASE DON'T BAN

THESE CARS NO MORE. BRING IT BACK
THE GOOD OLD DAYS.

WITH LOVE,
KAYING KHANG

MY DREAM DID NOT COME TRUE YET.
IM TRYING. HAHAHAHAHAAHAHHAHA
BILLLIONS OF DOLLARS IS COMING TO
YOU AND ME. AHAHAHAHA MAKE
MONEY FLOW TO ME AND YOU! BE
SECURED. FOLLOW YOUR HEART!

LOVE,
PEACE,
LOVE,
PEACE,
LOVE, PEACE. THE END. MAKE MONEY!

This second print in this book is meant for you to read it again and plus I needed 24 pages to print the books for you.

Thank you everyone! Have a nice life. I love you too. Gods bless us all. Merry Christmas! Happy New Years! HAPPY BIRTHDAYS! Or just Enjoy a Beautiful Day!

Good bye now. ☺

We have to READ the Book Again. Mind as well because my computer program I used is KINDLE DIRECT / AMAZON to publish this book. And you can make book for yourself too with Microsoft Word applications to write it type and upload it on your made account on Kindle / Amazon. So we have to read this book again okay? Okay. Here we go…I needed 79 pages to publish my book so here's the third time to read it through. Sorry. You don't have to read it so many times. Just skip through it or something….just don't read it but Thank you for buying my book. With love, Kaying.

READ

THIS

BOOK.

Author: KAYING
KHANG

TODAY'S DATE:
FEBRUARY 9, 2024.

THIS BOOK IS FOR
YOU WHO SEEKS A
SELF-HELP BOOK.

READ ON TO DISCOVER SOMETHING
OLD OR NEW FOR YOUR MIND AND LIFE.

Once Upon a Time in a Land Long Ago, there
lived a man and his wife and his family and
childrens.

A world where everything matters and only
KINDNESS is the key to ultimate success and
freedoms on Earth.

There was a MISSION for all Humans to come
down to Earth by Birth for a Vision we see and

know and do! KARMA good and bad endows all.

It is eminent to say that 'YO WHATS UP BITCH!' "YOU SEE I GOT MONEY" "NO MAN IM BROKE!"

AND THERE WAS ONCE A FAIRY TALE. But that Dream died when True Love Prevailed.

And now ancient as history, this book lives to tell you the WAYS to LIFE.

What is LIVING you might ask? It is not just breathing Air or Oxygen but it is in sense, the freedom to live with your life values in Good Man's worlds. With "pursuit of life, love, liberty and freedom."

Now as a child, I did and do PLEDGE MY ALLIGIANCE. I am glad to be part of this world and a country of love and freedom.

But I worry everyday because I'm broke. HOW DO I GET RICH NOW AT 43 NOW THAT OPPORTUNITIES ARE AT STAKE??? 2024 IS MY YEAR.

I MIGHT NEVER BE RICH BUT I HOPE I MAKE SOME INCOME. SO I WROTE THIS BOOK.

I have no mentor except this voice on youtube atm. 'FINANCIAL PROSPERITY IS MY STATE OF BEING. I AM GRATEFUL FOR THE ABUNDANCE THAT SURROUNDS ME. I AM READY FOR THE …. THE UNIVERSE …I AM A MONEY MAGNET ATTRACTING WEALTH EFFORTLESSLY. … FINANCIAL

OPPORTUNITIES….I AM A POWERFUL CREATOR OF WEALTH AND SUCCESS. …I ATTRACT WEALTH BY ALIGNING MY ACTIONS WITH MY GOALS. I AM OPEN TO RECEIVING UNLIMITED PROSPERITY. …"

THERE that was the KEY TO WEALTH YOU JUST READ AND HEARD but it is not the only way.

MONEY IS FREE TO RECEIVE AS RESOURCES MADE WERE FREE. ON EARTH AND BY HUMANS.

ONLY THE BEARED LABOR MADE THINGS COSTED MONEY BECAUSE SOMEDAY BROUGHT IT OUT TO US ALL BY THEIR HANDS AND BRAINS AND WORK, LABORS.

SO THUS OUR LITTLE FREE WORLD COSTS MONEY BECAUSE WE ARE ALL STRANGERS AND COULD NOT YET GIVE FREELY BACK ONE DAY YET TODAY EVEN IN YEAR 2024 WORLD WIDE.

THUS MONEY HAD TO BE THE LETTER OF TRUST TO MAKE THE BARTER PAID TO ITS SOURCES THAT BROUGHT US THRU FRUIT AND WORK, THE LABOR THAT BROUGHT US ALL THESE BEAUTIFUL THINGS IN THIS WONDERFUL WORLD(s).

In my world, I got everything for free yet I had to pay things with money that I got for free but now that im 43 I need more money. I DO WANT TO BECOME A TRILLIONAIRE! But this is only a DREAM for now.

It is hard to be RICH because I do not want to be a target to be outlisted or a public profile where Poparrizzis follow me daily. Gosh that's no life at all! Anyone?

Wont even be able to walk into the Mall no more to buy my shoes or clothes than! Hahahaahah that's not good.

So this book is intended to help you and all everythone to become RICH millions billions Trillions QuadtripleTrillions!!!??? Who knows….we can do this right? People mastered the skills of being rich. Why not you and me.

But the secret is this kids! MONEY WAS GIVEN TO HALF THE RICH TO BE KEPT RICH FREELY. Nobody told me that government and countries can give people

money to be rich by GRANTS, LOANS,
INCOME, PROFITS! ETC….

WELL THE KEY IS TO WEALTH IS
ABUNDANCE TO LIFE IS SECURITY TO
LOVE AND LIVE WITH FEES FREEDOME.

"WHO WANTS TO BE A LITTLE
millionaire?" Some KIDS FIGURED IT OUT.
SOME NEVER GAVE THEMSELVES A FAIR
CHANCE SO THIS BOOK SAYS IF YOU
CAN THINK IT, IF YOU CAN DREAM AND
BELIEVE IN IT AND NO ONE IS HURTING
YOU, YOU ARE FREE TO MAKE BILLIONS
MILLIONS TRILLIONS BUT PEOPLE JUST
DON'T KNOW ALL THAT MONEY FOR
WHAT?

Heck I still don't know…im just trying to find a
way to pay our mortgage and get food and buy a

cheap car I can drive again with paid insurance, etc…im the most broke joke blow it all lost B in America. I swear. Man….my life is hard. Because people are hating on me with their conspiracy Joni R and them drugging me 20 years for bad records of mental illness… I thought I was second class medicine/ citizen being Hmong so I accepted their tortures on my life 20 years but today I write my book to tell the world, WE CAN ALL BE BILLIONAIRES.

THEY KNEW IM SET TO BE RICH BUT NOW IM DIRT POOR BECAUSE THEY DRUGGED ME TOO LONG IN DRUGS THAT WILL RETARD ME AND IM WORKING WITH TIME NOW BEFORE MY LITTLE BODY GIVES OUT TO THEIR DRUGS ANYMORE! JONI R THEY ARE ENDANGERING MY LIFE WITH MENTALLY ILL DRUGS ON PURPOSE IN THEIR TARGET TO WRONGFULLY KILL

ME BECAUSE JONI had sex with my brother on accident in Nekoosa WISCONSIN when we are in Elementary school playgrounds 3x 4 x Joni told me that day on the play ground. Heck I did not even know I had a brother til later. I am sorry okay. I'm sorry. Please do not hurt me anymore Joni Redepeening/Reimber aka Lyndsey.

With Love,

Kaying Khang.

So??? The right path to "financial success?" That's this:

4. Either get a JOB work by the hour for money get paid x days or a week(s) later
5. Or Work for somebody or make your own companies to build somethings to offers some services and sales from those two options for your company.

6. Get loans to run a business. Business can be in ANY LEGAL SECTORS / INDUSTRIES. YOU can DREAM here and make your visions become true but I advise do it legally. That is do not steal, no crimes and open run your operations legally to profit sales and revenue into your business. For profit or nonprofit type businesses. Google it up: the difference between a profit or nonprofit business.

To me? They are the same things PROFITS and NONPROFITS. EXCEPT in their BOOK KEEPING ACCOUNTING RECORDS ARE CLASSIFIED JUST A LITTLE DIFFERENLY. THEY BOTH MAKE MILLIONS BILLIONS DOLLARS OR can both be in DEFICIT TOO/ loss incomes.

THERE THAT'S THE KEY TO MAKING
MONEY FOR YOURSELF!

NOW, WHAT KIND OF CAR DO YOU WANT
TO DRIVE AS A MILIONARIE?

HMMM I ALWAYS THOUGHT IT THE
LAMBOURGHINI BUT I THINK THAT'S
MADE IN ITALY AND IM NOT SURE
EVERYONE WANTS TO DRIVE THAT CAR
RIGHT???? JK, MYSELF I DON'T WANT TO
DRIVE THAT KIND OF CAR ITS TOO
HARD.

EVEN IF I WERE RICH I'LL DRIVE AN OLD
NICE IMPORTS PLEASE DON'T BAN
THESE CARS NO MORE. BRING IT BACK
THE GOOD OLD DAYS.

WITH LOVE,
KAYING KHANG

MY DREAM DID NOT COME TRUE YET.
IM TRYING. HAHAHAHAHAAHAHHAHA
BILLLIONS OF DOLLARS IS COMING TO
YOU AND ME. AHAHAHAHA MAKE
MONEY FLOW TO ME AND YOU! BE
SECURED. FOLLOW YOUR HEART!

LOVE,

PEACE,

LOVE,

PEACE,

LOVE, PEACE. THE END. MAKE MONEY!

READ

THIS

BOOK.

Author: KAYING KHANG

TODAY'S DATE:
FEBRUARY 9, 2024.

THIS BOOK IS FOR
YOU WHO SEEKS A
SELF-HELP BOOK.

READ ON TO DISCOVER SOMETHING
OLD OR NEW FOR YOUR MIND AND LIFE.

Once Upon a Time in a Land Long Ago, there lived a man and his wife and his family and childrens.

A world where everything matters and only KINDNESS is the key to ultimate success and freedoms on Earth.

There was a MISSION for all Humans to come down to Earth by Birth for a Vision we see and know and do! KARMA good and bad endows all.

It is eminent to say that 'YO WHATS UP BITCH!' "YOU SEE I GOT MONEY" "NO MAN IM BROKE!"

AND THERE WAS ONCE A FAIRY TALE. But that Dream died when True Love Prevailed.

And now ancient as history, this book lives to tell you the WAYS to LIFE.

What is LIVING you might ask? It is not just breathing Air or Oxygen but it is in sense, the freedom to live with your life values in Good Man's worlds. With "pursuit of life, love, liberty and freedom."

Now as a child, I did and do PLEDGE MY ALLIGIANCE. I am glad to be part of this world and a country of love and freedom.

But I worry everyday because I'm broke. HOW DO I GET RICH NOW AT 43 NOW THAT OPPORTUNITIES ARE AT STAKE??? 2024 IS MY YEAR.

I MIGHT NEVER BE RICH BUT I HOPE I MAKE SOME INCOME. SO I WROTE THIS BOOK.

I have no mentor except this voice on youtube atm. 'FINANCIAL PROSPERITY IS MY STATE OF BEING. I AM GRATEFUL FOR THE ABUNDANCE THAT SURROUNDS ME. I AM READY FOR THE …. THE UNIVERSE …I AM A MONEY MAGNET ATTRACTING WEALTH EFFORTLESSLY. … FINANCIAL OPPORTUNITIES….I AM A POWERFUL CREATOR OF WEALTH AND SUCCESS. …I ATTRACT WEALTH BY ALIGNING MY ACTIONS WITH MY GOALS. I AM OPEN TO RECEIVING UNLIMITED PROSPERITY. …"

THERE that was the KEY TO WEALTH YOU JUST READ AND HEARD but it is not the only way.

MONEY IS FREE TO RECEIVE AS
RESOURCES MADE WERE FREE. ON
EARTH AND BY HUMANS.

ONLY THE BEARED LABOR MADE
THINGS COSTED MONEY BECAUSE
SOMEDAY BROUGHT IT OUT TO US ALL
BY THEIR HANDS AND BRAINS AND
WORK, LABORS.

SO THUS OUR LITTLE FREE WORLD
COSTS MONEY BECAUSE WE ARE ALL
STRANGERS AND COULD NOT YET GIVE
FREELY BACK ONE DAY YET TODAY
EVEN IN YEAR 2024 WORLD WIDE.

THUS MONEY HAD TO BE THE LETTER
OF TRUST TO MAKE THE BARTER PAID
TO ITS SOURCES THAT BROUGHT US
THRU FRUIT AND WORK, THE LABOR

THAT BROUGHT US ALL THESE BEAUTIFUL THINGS IN THIS WONDERFUL WORLD(s).

In my world, I got everything for free yet I had to pay things with money that I got for free but now that im 43 I need more money. I DO WANT TO BECOME A TRILLIONAIRE! But this is only a DREAM for now.

It is hard to be RICH because I do not want to be a target to be outlisted or a public profile where Poparrizzis follow me daily. Gosh that's no life at all! Anyone?

Wont even be able to walk into the Mall no more to buy my shoes or clothes than! Hahahaahah that's not good.

So this book is intended to help you and all everythone to become RICH millions billions Trillions QuadtripleTrillions!!!??? Who knows….we can do this right? People mastered the skills of being rich. Why not you and me.

But the secret is this kids! MONEY WAS GIVEN TO HALF THE RICH TO BE KEPT RICH FREELY. Nobody told me that government and countries can give people money to be rich by GRANTS, LOANS, INCOME, PROFITS! ETC….

WELL THE KEY IS TO WEALTH IS ABUNDANCE TO LIFE IS SECURITY TO LOVE AND LIVE WITH FEES FREEDOME.

"WHO WANTS TO BE A LITTLE millionaire?" Some KIDS FIGURED IT OUT. SOME NEVER GAVE THEMSELVES A FAIR

CHANCE SO THIS BOOK SAYS IF YOU CAN THINK IT, IF YOU CAN DREAM AND BELIEVE IN IT AND NO ONE IS HURTING YOU, YOU ARE FREE TO MAKE BILLIONS MILLIONS TRILLIONS BUT PEOPLE JUST DON'T KNOW ALL THAT MONEY FOR WHAT?

Heck I still don't know…im just trying to find a way to pay our mortgage and get food and buy a cheap car I can drive again with paid insurance, etc…im the most broke joke blow it all lost B in America. I swear. Man….my life is hard. Because people are hating on me with their conspiracy Joni R and them drugging me 20 years for bad records of mental illness… I thought I was second class medicine/ citizen being Hmong so I accepted their tortures on my life 20 years but today I write my book to tell the world, WE CAN ALL BE BILLIONAIRES.

THEY KNEW IM SET TO BE RICH BUT NOW IM DIRT POOR BECAUSE THEY DRUGGED ME TOO LONG IN DRUGS THAT WILL RETARD ME AND IM WORKING WITH TIME NOW BEFORE MY LITTLE BODY GIVES OUT TO THEIR DRUGS ANYMORE! JONI R THEY ARE ENDANGERING MY LIFE WITH MENTALLY ILL DRUGS ON PURPOSE IN THEIR TARGET TO WRONGFULLY KILL ME BECAUSE JONI had sex with my brother on accident in Nekoosa WISCONSIN when we are in Elementary school playgrounds 3x 4 x Joni told me that day on the play ground. Heck I did not even know I had a brother til later. I am sorry okay. I'm sorry. Please do not hurt me anymore Joni Redepeening/Reimber aka Lyndsey.

With Love,
Kaying Khang.

So??? The right path to "financial success?"
That's this:

4. Either get a JOB work by the hour for
   money get paid x days or a week(s) later
5. Or Work for somebody or make your own
   companies to build somethings to offers
   some services and sales from those two
   options for your company.
6. Get loans to run a business. Business can
   be in ANY LEGAL SECTORS /
   INDUSTRIES. YOU can DREAM here and
   make your visions become true but I advise
   do it legally. That is do not steal, no crimes
   and open run your operations legally to
   profit sales and revenue into your business.
   For profit or nonprofit type businesses.
   Google it up: the difference between a
   profit or nonprofit business.

To me? They are the same things PROFITS and
NONPROFITS. EXCEPT in their BOOK

KEEPING ACCOUNTING RECORDS ARE CLASSIFIED JUST A LITTLE DIFFERENLY. THEY BOTH MAKE MILLIONS BILLIONS DOLLARS OR can both be in DEFICIT TOO/ loss incomes.

THERE THAT'S THE KEY TO MAKING MONEY FOR YOURSELF!

NOW, WHAT KIND OF CAR DO YOU WANT TO DRIVE AS A MILIONARIE?

HMMM I ALWAYS THOUGHT IT THE LAMBOURGIIINI BUT I THINK THAT'S MADE IN ITALY AND IM NOT SURE EVERYONE WANTS TO DRIVE THAT CAR RIGHT???? JK, MYSELF I DON'T WANT TO DRIVE THAT KIND OF CAR ITS TOO HARD.

EVEN IF I WERE RICH I'LL DRIVE AN OLD NICE IMPORTS PLEASE DON'T BAN

THESE CARS NO MORE. BRING IT BACK
THE GOOD OLD DAYS.

WITH LOVE,
KAYING KHANG

MY DREAM DID NOT COME TRUE YET.
IM TRYING. HAHAHAHAHAAHAHHAHA
BILLLIONS OF DOLLARS IS COMING TO
YOU AND ME. AHAHAHAHA MAKE
MONEY FLOW TO ME AND YOU! BE
SECURED. FOLLOW YOUR HEART!

LOVE,
PEACE,
LOVE,
PEACE,
LOVE, PEACE. THE END. MAKE MONEY!

This second print in this book is meant for you to read it again and plus I needed 24 pages to print the books for you.

Thank you everyone! Have a nice life. I love you too. Gods bless us all. Merry Christmas! Happy New Years! HAPPY BIRTHDAYS! Or just Enjoy a Beautiful Day!

Good bye now. 😊

I'm still short on my little book, sorry its too lame. If it helped your life, GREAT! I'm not sure how I'll get to be rich yet too???!!!

READ THIS BOOK.

Author: KAYING KHANG

TODAY'S DATE:
FEBRUARY 9, 2024.

THIS BOOK IS FOR
YOU WHO SEEKS A
SELF-HELP BOOK.

READ ON TO DISCOVER SOMETHING
OLD OR NEW FOR YOUR MIND AND LIFE.

Once Upon a Time in a Land Long Ago, there lived a man and his wife and his family and childrens.

A world where everything matters and only KINDNESS is the key to ultimate success and freedoms on Earth.

There was a MISSION for all Humans to come down to Earth by Birth for a Vision we see and know and do! KARMA good and bad endows all.

It is eminent to say that 'YO WHATS UP BITCH!' "YOU SEE I GOT MONEY" "NO MAN IM BROKE!"

AND THERE WAS ONCE A FAIRY TALE. But that Dream died when True Love Prevailed.

And now ancient as history, this book lives to tell you the WAYS to LIFE.

What is LIVING you might ask? It is not just breathing Air or Oxygen but it is in sense, the freedom to live with your life values in Good Man's worlds. With "pursuit of life, love, liberty and freedom."

Now as a child, I did and do PLEDGE MY ALLIGIANCE. I am glad to be part of this world and a country of love and freedom.

But I worry everyday because I'm broke. HOW DO I GET RICH NOW AT 43 NOW THAT OPPORTUNITIES ARE AT STAKE??? 2024 IS MY YEAR.

I MIGHT NEVER BE RICH BUT I HOPE I MAKE SOME INCOME. SO I WROTE THIS BOOK.

I have no mentor except this voice on youtube atm. 'FINANCIAL PROSPERITY IS MY STATE OF BEING. I AM GRATEFUL FOR THE ABUNDANCE THAT SURROUNDS ME. I AM READY FOR THE …. THE UNIVERSE …I AM A MONEY MAGNET ATTRACTING WEALTH EFFORTLESSLY. … FINANCIAL OPPORTUNITIES….I AM A POWERFUL CREATOR OF WEALTH AND SUCCESS. …I ATTRACT WEALTH BY ALIGNING MY ACTIONS WITH MY GOALS. I AM OPEN TO RECEIVING UNLIMITED PROSPERITY. …"

THERE that was the KEY TO WEALTH YOU JUST READ AND HEARD but it is not the only way.

MONEY IS FREE TO RECEIVE AS RESOURCES MADE WERE FREE. ON EARTH AND BY HUMANS.

ONLY THE BEARED LABOR MADE THINGS COSTED MONEY BECAUSE SOMEDAY BROUGHT IT OUT TO US ALL BY THEIR HANDS AND BRAINS AND WORK, LABORS.

SO THUS OUR LITTLE FREE WORLD COSTS MONEY BECAUSE WE ARE ALL STRANGERS AND COULD NOT YET GIVE FREELY BACK ONE DAY YET TODAY EVEN IN YEAR 2024 WORLD WIDE.

THUS MONEY HAD TO BE THE LETTER OF TRUST TO MAKE THE BARTER PAID TO ITS SOURCES THAT BROUGHT US THRU FRUIT AND WORK, THE LABOR

THAT BROUGHT US ALL THESE
BEAUTIFUL THINGS IN THIS
WONDERFUL WORLD(s).

In my world, I got everything for free yet I had
to pay things with money that I got for free but
now that im 43 I need more money. I DO
WANT TO BECOME A TRILLIONAIRE! But
this is only a DREAM for now.

It is hard to be RICH because I do not want to
be a target to be outlisted or a public profile
where Poparrizzis follow me daily. Gosh that's
no life at all! Anyone?

Wont even be able to walk into the Mall no
more to buy my shoes or clothes than!
Hahahaahah that's not good.

So this book is intended to help you and all everythone to become RICH millions billions Trillions QuadtripleTrillions!!!??? Who knows….we can do this right? People mastered the skills of being rich. Why not you and me.

But the secret is this kids! MONEY WAS GIVEN TO HALF THE RICH TO BE KEPT RICH FREELY. Nobody told me that government and countries can give people money to be rich by GRANTS, LOANS, INCOME, PROFITS! ETC….

WELL THE KEY IS TO WEALTH IS ABUNDANCE TO LIFE IS SECURITY TO LOVE AND LIVE WITH FEES FREEDOME.

"WHO WANTS TO BE A LITTLE millionaire?" Some KIDS FIGURED IT OUT. SOME NEVER GAVE THEMSELVES A FAIR

CHANCE SO THIS BOOK SAYS IF YOU CAN THINK IT, IF YOU CAN DREAM AND BELIEVE IN IT AND NO ONE IS HURTING YOU, YOU ARE FREE TO MAKE BILLIONS MILLIONS TRILLIONS BUT PEOPLE JUST DON'T KNOW ALL THAT MONEY FOR WHAT?

Heck I still don't know…im just trying to find a way to pay our mortgage and get food and buy a cheap car I can drive again with paid insurance, etc…im the most broke joke blow it all lost B in America. I swear. Man….my life is hard. Because people are hating on me with their conspiracy Joni R and them drugging me 20 years for bad records of mental illness… I thought I was second class medicine/ citizen being Hmong so I accepted their tortures on my life 20 years but today I write my book to tell the world, WE CAN ALL BE BILLIONAIRES.

THEY KNEW IM SET TO BE RICH BUT NOW IM DIRT POOR BECAUSE THEY DRUGGED ME TOO LONG IN DRUGS THAT WILL RETARD ME AND IM WORKING WITH TIME NOW BEFORE MY LITTLE BODY GIVES OUT TO THEIR DRUGS ANYMORE! JONI R THEY ARE ENDANGERING MY LIFE WITH MENTALLY ILL DRUGS ON PURPOSE IN THEIR TARGET TO WRONGFULLY KILL ME BECAUSE JONI had sex with my brother on accident in Nekoosa WISCONSIN when we are in Elementary school playgrounds 3x 4 x Joni told me that day on the play ground. Heck I did not even know I had a brother til later. I am sorry okay. I'm sorry. Please do not hurt me anymore Joni Redepeening/Reimber aka Lyndsey.

With Love,
Kaying Khang.

So??? The right path to "financial success?"
That's this:

7. Either get a JOB work by the hour for
   money get paid x days or a week(s) later
8. Or Work for somebody or make your own
   companies to build somethings to offers
   some services and sales from those two
   options for your company.
9. Get loans to run a business. Business can
   be in ANY LEGAL SECTORS /
   INDUSTRIES. YOU can DREAM here and
   make your visions become true but I advise
   do it legally. That is do not steal, no crimes
   and open run your operations legally to
   profit sales and revenue into your business.
   For profit or nonprofit type businesses.
   Google it up: the difference between a
   profit or nonprofit business.

To me? They are the same things PROFITS and
NONPROFITS. EXCEPT in their BOOK

KEEPING ACCOUNTING RECORDS ARE CLASSIFIED JUST A LITTLE DIFFERENLY. THEY BOTH MAKE MILLIONS BILLIONS DOLLARS OR can both be in DEFICIT TOO/ loss incomes.

THERE THAT'S THE KEY TO MAKING MONEY FOR YOURSELF!

NOW, WHAT KIND OF CAR DO YOU WANT TO DRIVE AS A MILIONARIE?

HMMM I ALWAYS THOUGHT IT THE LAMBOURGHINI BUT I THINK TIIAT'S MADE IN ITALY AND IM NOT SURE EVERYONE WANTS TO DRIVE THAT CAR RIGHT???? JK, MYSELF I DON'T WANT TO DRIVE THAT KIND OF CAR ITS TOO HARD.

EVEN IF I WERE RICH I'LL DRIVE AN OLD NICE IMPORTS PLEASE DON'T BAN

THESE CARS NO MORE. BRING IT BACK
THE GOOD OLD DAYS.

WITH LOVE,
KAYING KHANG

MY DREAM DID NOT COME TRUE YET.
IM TRYING. HAHAHAHAHAAHAHHAHA
BILLLIONS OF DOLLARS IS COMING TO
YOU AND ME. AHAHAHAHA MAKE
MONEY FLOW TO ME AND YOU! BE
SECURED. FOLLOW YOUR HEART!

LOVE,
PEACE,
LOVE,
PEACE,
LOVE, PEACE. THE END. MAKE MONEY!

READ

THIS

BOOK.

Author: KAYING KHANG

TODAY'S DATE:
FEBRUARY 9, 2024.

THIS BOOK IS FOR
YOU WHO SEEKS A
SELF-HELP BOOK.

READ ON TO DISCOVER SOMETHING
OLD OR NEW FOR YOUR MIND AND LIFE.

Once Upon a Time in a Land Long Ago, there lived a man and his wife and his family and childrens.

A world where everything matters and only KINDNESS is the key to ultimate success and freedoms on Earth.

There was a MISSION for all Humans to come down to Earth by Birth for a Vision we see and know and do! KARMA good and bad endows all.

It is eminent to say that 'YO WHATS UP BITCH!' "YOU SEE I GOT MONEY" "NO MAN IM BROKE!"

AND THERE WAS ONCE A FAIRY TALE. But that Dream died when True Love Prevailed.

And now ancient as history, this book lives to tell you the WAYS to LIFE.

What is LIVING you might ask? It is not just breathing Air or Oxygen but it is in sense, the freedom to live with your life values in Good Man's worlds. With "pursuit of life, love, liberty and freedom."

Now as a child, I did and do PLEDGE MY ALLIGIANCE. I am glad to be part of this world and a country of love and freedom.

But I worry everyday because I'm broke. HOW DO I GET RICH NOW AT 43 NOW THAT OPPORTUNITIES ARE AT STAKE??? 2024 IS MY YEAR.

I MIGHT NEVER BE RICH BUT I HOPE I MAKE SOME INCOME. SO I WROTE THIS BOOK.

I have no mentor except this voice on youtube atm. 'FINANCIAL PROSPERITY IS MY STATE OF BEING. I AM GRATEFUL FOR THE ABUNDANCE THAT SURROUNDS ME. I AM READY FOR THE …. THE UNIVERSE …I AM A MONEY MAGNET ATTRACTING WEALTH EFFORTLESSLY. … FINANCIAL OPPORTUNITIES….I AM A POWERFUL CREATOR OF WEALTH AND SUCCESS. …I ATTRACT WEALTH BY ALIGNING MY ACTIONS WITH MY GOALS. I AM OPEN TO RECEIVING UNLIMITED PROSPERITY. …"

THERE that was the KEY TO WEALTH YOU JUST READ AND HEARD but it is not the only way.

MONEY IS FREE TO RECEIVE AS
RESOURCES MADE WERE FREE. ON
EARTH AND BY HUMANS.

ONLY THE BEARED LABOR MADE
THINGS COSTED MONEY BECAUSE
SOMEDAY BROUGHT IT OUT TO US ALL
BY THEIR HANDS AND BRAINS AND
WORK, LABORS.

SO THUS OUR LITTLE FREE WORLD
COSTS MONEY BECAUSE WE ARE ALL
STRANGERS AND COULD NOT YET GIVE
FREELY BACK ONE DAY YET TODAY
EVEN IN YEAR 2024 WORLD WIDE.

THUS MONEY HAD TO BE THE LETTER
OF TRUST TO MAKE THE BARTER PAID
TO ITS SOURCES THAT BROUGHT US
THRU FRUIT AND WORK, THE LABOR

THAT BROUGHT US ALL THESE
BEAUTIFUL THINGS IN THIS
WONDERFUL WORLD(s).

In my world, I got everything for free yet I had
to pay things with money that I got for free but
now that im 43 I need more money. I DO
WANT TO BECOME A TRILLIONAIRE! But
this is only a DREAM for now.

It is hard to be RICH because I do not want to
be a target to be outlisted or a public profile
where Poparrizzis follow me daily. Gosh that's
no life at all! Anyone?

Wont even be able to walk into the Mall no
more to buy my shoes or clothes than!
Hahahaahah that's not good.

So this book is intended to help you and all everythone to become RICH millions billions Trillions QuadtripleTrillions!!!??? Who knows….we can do this right? People mastered the skills of being rich. Why not you and me.

But the secret is this kids! MONEY WAS GIVEN TO HALF THE RICH TO BE KEPT RICH FREELY. Nobody told me that government and countries can give people money to be rich by GRANTS, LOANS, INCOME, PROFITS! ETC….

WELL THE KEY IS TO WEALTH IS ABUNDANCE TO LIFE IS SECURITY TO LOVE AND LIVE WITH FEES FREEDOME.

"WHO WANTS TO BE A LITTLE millionaire?" Some KIDS FIGURED IT OUT. SOME NEVER GAVE THEMSELVES A FAIR

CHANCE SO THIS BOOK SAYS IF YOU CAN THINK IT, IF YOU CAN DREAM AND BELIEVE IN IT AND NO ONE IS HURTING YOU, YOU ARE FREE TO MAKE BILLIONS MILLIONS TRILLIONS BUT PEOPLE JUST DON'T KNOW ALL THAT MONEY FOR WHAT?

Heck I still don't know…im just trying to find a way to pay our mortgage and get food and buy a cheap car I can drive again with paid insurance, etc…im the most broke joke blow it all lost B in America. I swear. Man….my life is hard. Because people are hating on me with their conspiracy Joni R and them drugging me 20 years for bad records of mental illness… I thought I was second class medicine/ citizen being Hmong so I accepted their tortures on my life 20 years but today I write my book to tell the world, WE CAN ALL BE BILLIONAIRES.

THEY KNEW IM SET TO BE RICH BUT NOW IM DIRT POOR BECAUSE THEY DRUGGED ME TOO LONG IN DRUGS THAT WILL RETARD ME AND IM WORKING WITH TIME NOW BEFORE MY LITTLE BODY GIVES OUT TO THEIR DRUGS ANYMORE! JONI R THEY ARE ENDANGERING MY LIFE WITH MENTALLY ILL DRUGS ON PURPOSE IN THEIR TARGET TO WRONGFULLY KILL ME BECAUSE JONI had sex with my brother on accident in Nekoosa WISCONSIN when we are in Elementary school playgrounds 3x 4 x Joni told me that day on the play ground. Heck I did not even know I had a brother til later. I am sorry okay. I'm sorry. Please do not hurt me anymore Joni Redepeening/Reimber aka Lyndsey.

With Love,
Kaying Khang.

So??? The right path to "financial success?"
That's this:

7. Either get a JOB work by the hour for money get paid x days or a week(s) later
8. Or Work for somebody or make your own companies to build somethings to offers some services and sales from those two options for your company.
9. Get loans to run a business. Business can be in ANY LEGAL SECTORS / INDUSTRIES. YOU can DREAM here and make your visions become true but I advise do it legally. That is do not steal, no crimes and open run your operations legally to profit sales and revenue into your business. For profit or nonprofit type businesses. Google it up: the difference between a profit or nonprofit business.

To me? They are the same things PROFITS and NONPROFITS. EXCEPT in their BOOK

KEEPING ACCOUNTING RECORDS ARE CLASSIFIED JUST A LITTLE DIFFERENLY. THEY BOTH MAKE MILLIONS BILLIONS DOLLARS OR can both be in DEFICIT TOO/ loss incomes.

THERE THAT'S THE KEY TO MAKING MONEY FOR YOURSELF!

NOW, WHAT KIND OF CAR DO YOU WANT TO DRIVE AS A MILIONARIE?

HMMM I ALWAYS THOUGHT IT THE LAMBOURGHINI BUT I THINK THAT'S MADE IN ITALY AND IM NOT SURE EVERYONE WANTS TO DRIVE THAT CAR RIGHT???? JK, MYSELF I DON'T WANT TO DRIVE THAT KIND OF CAR ITS TOO HARD.

EVEN IF I WERE RICH I'LL DRIVE AN OLD NICE IMPORTS PLEASE DON'T BAN

THESE CARS NO MORE. BRING IT BACK
THE GOOD OLD DAYS.

WITH LOVE,
KAYING KHANG

MY DREAM DID NOT COME TRUE YET.
IM TRYING. HAHAHAHAHAAHAHHAHA
BILLLIONS OF DOLLARS IS COMING TO
YOU AND ME. AHAHAHAHA MAKE
MONEY FLOW TO ME AND YOU! BE
SECURED. FOLLOW YOUR HEART!

LOVE,
PEACE,
LOVE,
PEACE,
LOVE, PEACE. THE END. MAKE MONEY!

This second print in this book is meant for you to read it again and plus I needed 24 pages to print the books for you.

Thank you everyone! Have a nice life. I love you too. Gods bless us all. Merry Christmas! Happy New Years! HAPPY BIRTHDAYS! Or just Enjoy a Beautiful Day!

Good bye now. ☺

There done! 82 pages. Yeah! All done. Time to go now. I"ll write another book another day. Sleep well and make dreams come true! Be good and enjoy a Beautiful day! Bye bye now.